Science
from the beginning

Science
from the beginning

B L Hampson and K C Evans

Pupils' Book 1

Oliver & Boyd

OLIVER & BOYD
Robert Stevenson House
Baxter's Place
Leith Walk
Edinburgh EH1 3BB

A Division of Longman Group Limited

First published 1960
New Edition 1976
Ninth impression 1985

ISBN 0 05 002907 X

Produced by Longman Group (F.E.) Ltd
Printed in Hong Kong

CONTENTS

CONTENTS

CONTENTS

THE THREE KINDS OF THINGS

* There are three kinds of things in the world.
* Some of them are living now.
  We call these ALIVE.
* Some of them have been alive and have died.
  We call these DEAD.
* All the others have never been alive.
  We shall call these NEVER ALIVE.
* If we had three giant boxes, we could give them
  names like this :

* If the boxes were big enough, we could put
  all the things in the world into them.
* The living things would go into the ALIVE box.
* The dead things would go into the DEAD box.
  All the rest would go into the NEVER ALIVE box.
* When you see a yellow spot in this book, like this,
  you will know that that page (or that part of
  the page) is about NEVER ALIVE things.

FOR YOU TO DRAW

ALIVE	DEAD	NEVER ALIVE

The three kinds of things

FOR YOU TO DO

1 Find out where lots of things you know would go.
2 Collect things for your science table.
3 Sort them into three sets on the science table.

ALIVE

DEAD

NEVER ALIVE

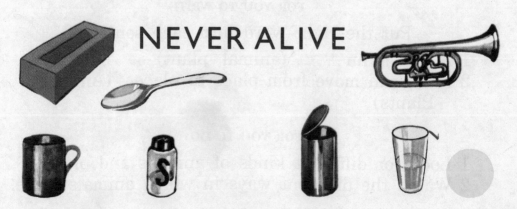

9

THE TWO KINDS OF LIVING THINGS

* There are two kinds of living things.

* Some grow in one place.
They cannot get up and go away.
They are called PLANTS.

* You will never see a tree walking about.
A tree is a PLANT.

* Other living things can move away to another place.
They are called ANIMALS.

* A fish can move from one place to another place.
A fish is an ANIMAL.

* You can move from one place to another place.
You are an ANIMAL.

* When you see a red spot in this book, like this,
you will know that that page (or that part of
the page) is about ANIMALS.
A green spot means it is about PLANTS.

FOR YOU TO DRAW

| LIVING ANIMALS | DEAD | NEVER |
| LIVING PLANTS | THINGS | ALIVE |

There are two kinds of living things.

FOR YOU TO WRITE

Put the right word into each sentence.

1 A fish is an ..... (animal, plant)
2 ..... can move from place to place. (Animals,
Plants)

FOR YOU TO DO

1 Look for different kinds of animals and plants.
2 Watch the different ways in which animals move.

ANIMALS

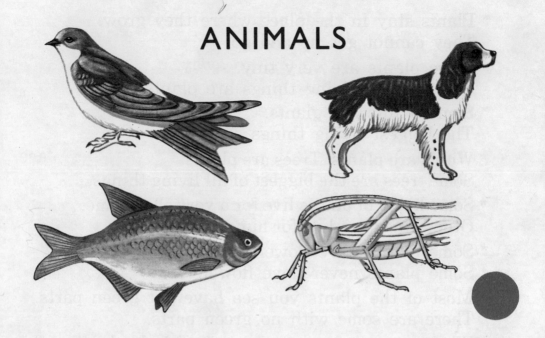

PLANTS

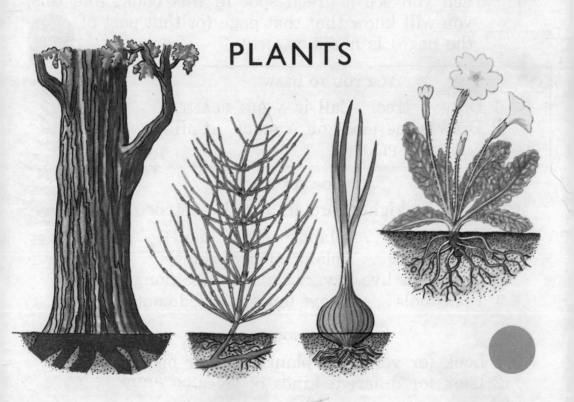

LIVING THINGS THAT CANNOT MOVE AWAY

* Plants stay in the place where they grow.
  They cannot get up and go.
* Some plants are very tiny.
  The smallest living things are plants.
* Some plants are giants.
  The biggest living things are plants.
* Weeds are plants. Trees are plants.
  Some trees are the biggest of all living things.
* Some kinds of plants live for a very short time.
  Other kinds can live for hundreds of years.
* Some plants have flowers.
  Some plants never have flowers.
* Most of the plants you see have got green parts.
  There are some with no green parts.
* When you see a green spot in this book, like this,
  you will know that that page (or that part of
  the page) is about PLANTS.

FOR YOU TO DRAW

1 Draw a tree. Call it A BIG PLANT.
2 Draw some moss on a stone. Call
  it TINY PLANTS.

FOR YOU TO WRITE

Put the right word into each sentence
1 Trees are . . . . . plants. (tiny, giant)
2 Moss is a . . . . . plant. (tiny, giant)
3 Trees can live a very . . . . . time. (long, short)
4 Toadstools . . . . . have flowers. (do, do not)

FIR TREE

FOR YOU TO DO

1 Look for very tiny plants and for bigger ones.
2 Look for different kinds of trees.

TINY PLANTS TO GIANT PLANTS

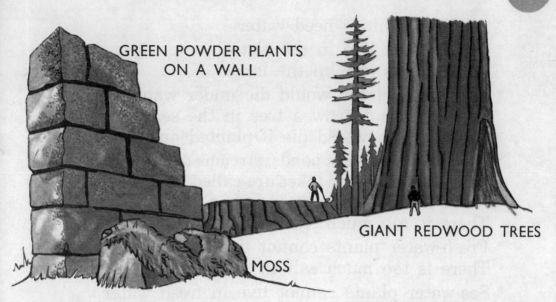

GREEN POWDER PLANTS
ON A WALL

GIANT REDWOOD TREES

MOSS

SOME PLANTS ARE TINY   SOME ARE VERY BIG

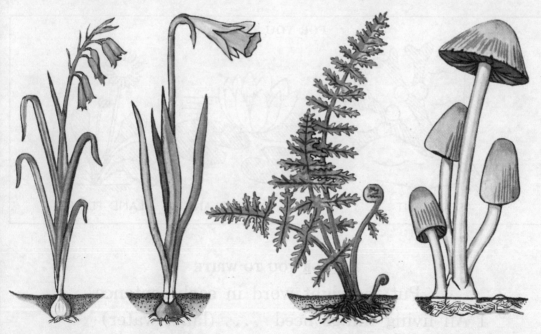

BLUEBELL   DAFFODIL   FERN   TOADSTOOL

SOME PLANTS HAVE FLOWERS   SOME HAVE NONE

THE HOMES OF PLANTS

* All living things need water.
* Some plants live in the water.
  Some plants live on the land.
* Most land plants would die under water.
  You could not grow a tree in the sea.
  Water plants would die if planted on the land.
* Many plants live in ponds, streams or lakes.
  Ponds, streams and lakes are called *fresh* water.
* We do not drink *sea* water.
  There is too much salt in it for us.
* Fresh-water plants cannot live in sea water.
  There is too much salt in it for them.
* Sea-water plants cannot live in fresh water.
  There is not enough salt in fresh water for them.
* Sea water plants never have flowers.

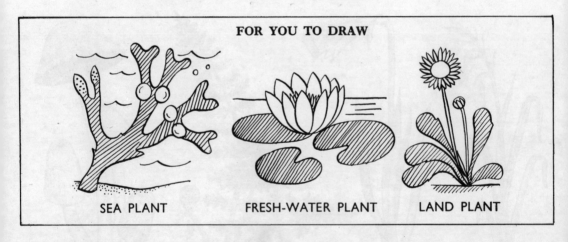

FOR YOU TO DRAW

SEA PLANT   FRESH-WATER PLANT   LAND PLANT

FOR YOU TO WRITE

Put the right word in each sentence.

1 All living things need . . . . . (land, water)
2 We drink . . . . . (sea water, fresh water)
3 There is more . . . . . in sea water. (land, salt)
4 Trees live on . . . . . (sea water, fresh water, land)

WHERE PLANTS LIVE

SOME PLANTS LIVE IN THE SEA

SOME PLANTS LIVE ON THE LAND

SOME PLANTS LIVE IN FRESH WATER

FOR YOU TO DO

1 When you are at the seaside, collect seaweeds of different colours.
2 Look for fresh-water plants that float, and ones that grow right out of the water.
3 Look for fresh-water plants that grow underneath the water.

ANIMAL SIZES, SHAPES AND COLOURS

* Different kinds of animals have different sizes.
  Some kinds are as tiny as a pin-point.
  Some, like elephants and whales, are huge.
* Different kinds of animals have different shapes.
  These shapes are made of body parts.
  Legs, arms wings, beaks and fins are body parts.
  So are heads, tails, hands and feet.
  Some parts are inside bodies.
  They cannot be seen.
* Shapes of animals suit their way of living.
* Different animals have different coloured bodies.
  Some have colours to match where they live
  These animals are not always easily seen.
* Some animals have bright colours.
  Often bright colours are warning colours.
  They warn enemies to keep away.

FOR YOU TO DRAW

Three different animal shapes

FOR YOU TO WRITE

Put the right word in each sentence.

1 Some animals are tiny, some are . . . . . (fat, huge)
2 Our bodies have . . . . . (arms, wings)
3 Animal shapes are made up of body . . . . . (parts, legs)
4 Bright colours warn . . . . . to keep away. (friends, enemies)

FOR YOU TO DO

1 Look for animals with warning colours.
2 Look at the shape of birds that live in bushes.
3 Look at the shape of birds that fly high in the sky.
4 Look at the different shapes of animals living in water. Some of these can be watched in an aquarium.

DIFFERENT SIZES

DIFFERENT SHAPES

DIFFERENT COLOURS

ANIMALS WITH HAIR

* All MAMMALS have hair.
  Many mammals use their hair to keep warm.
* When a mammal has a lot of hair, we call it FUR.
  All animals with fur are called mammals.
* Some mammals have short hairs on their bodies.
  They have found other ways of keeping warm.
  We have short hairs on our bodies.
  We are mammals.
  We wear clothes to keep warm.
  All baby mammals feed on milk.
* You still drink milk every day.
* Nearly every mammal has four limbs.
* Most mammals have tails.
  We are mammals without tails.

FOR YOU TO DRAW

Draw a mammal and write its name underneath.

FOR YOU TO WRITE

Put the right word into each sentence.

1 All baby mammals feed on ..... (ink, milk)
2 All mammals grow ..... (scales, hair, feathers)
3 Most mammals have ..... limbs. (six, four, ten)
4 I belong to the ..... class. (mammal, bird)

FOR YOU TO DO

1 If you go to the zoo, find out which mammals have a
  few hairs and which have enough to call fur.
2 See if you can collect loose hairs from
  some mammals.
  Stick them in your notebook with tape.

MAMMAL HAIRS

CAT   DOG   ME

3 Find out what different mammals eat.

MAMMALS

HAMSTER

GORILLA

BEAR

A LOT OF HAIR IS CALLED FUR

ELEPHANT

HUMANS

LION

ALL BABY MAMMALS FEED ON MILK

THE BAT IS THE ONLY
MAMMAL WHICH
CAN FLY

THE KANGAROO CARRIES
ITS BABY IN A POUCH

THE WALRUS LIVES
IN SEA WATER

ANIMALS WITH FEATHERS

* All animals with feathers are called BIRDS.
Every bird has feathers.
Feathers help to keep birds warm.
* Every bird has two wings.
Wings and feathers help a bird to fly.
* The swan, the crow and the gull live in Britain.
They all use their wings to fly.
* The ostrich and the penguin do not use their wings
to fly.
* The ostrich is the largest bird in the world.
Its wings are used to help it to run fast.
* The penguin feeds on fish.
Its wings are used to help it to swim.
* Every bird has two legs.
* Most birds have four toes on each foot.
Some birds have only three toes on each foot.
Some ostriches have only two toes on each foot.
* Birds lay eggs. Eggs are laid in nests.

FOR YOU TO DRAW

A BIRD'S EGG

A FEATHER

FOR YOU TO WRITE

Put the right word into each sentence.

1 Animals with feathers are called . . . . . (mammals, birds)
2 . . . . . keep a bird warm. (Hairs, Feathers, Scales)
3 Birds have . . . . . legs. (two, four, six)
4 Birds have . . . . . wings. (two, four, six)

BIRDS

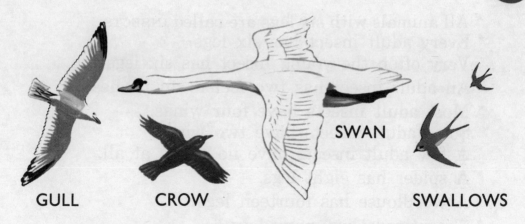

GULL   CROW   SWAN   SWALLOWS

SOME BIRDS USE THEIR WINGS TO FLY

OSTRICH

PENGUINS

SOME BIRDS DO NOT USE THEIR WINGS TO FLY

FOR YOU TO DO

1 Make a collection of feathers from different birds.
2 Look for gulls feeding away from the sea.
3 Look at a bird's beak, and look at its feet.

8

* All animals with six legs are called INSECTS.
* Every adult insect has six legs.
  Very often the young insect has six legs too.
* An adult insect has two feelers on its head.
* Most adult insects have four wings.
  Some adult insects have two wings.
  A few adult insects have no wings at all.
* A spider has eight legs.
* A woodlouse has fourteen legs.
* A centipede has many legs.
* The spider, the woodlouse and the centipede are NOT
  insects. They are other kinds of animals.
* The spider, the woodlouse and the centipede have no
  wings.

FOR YOU TO DRAW

An adult insect has six legs.

FOR YOU TO WRITE

Put the right word into each sentence.

1 An adult insect has . . . . . legs. (two, six, eight)
2 An adult insect has . . . . . feelers. (two, four, six)
3 Its feelers are on its . . . . . (body, wings, head)
4 A spider has . . . . . legs. (four, six, eight)

FOR YOU TO DO

1 Count the legs of every insect you see.
2 Look for the two feelers on its head.
3 See if you can find out how many wings it has.

INSECTS

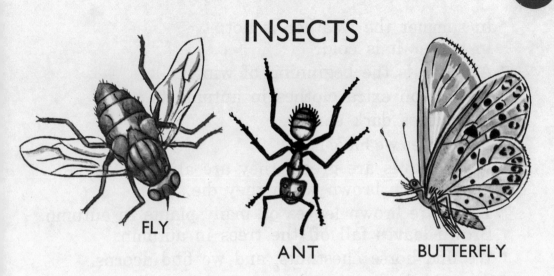

FLY

ANT

BUTTERFLY

NOT INSECTS

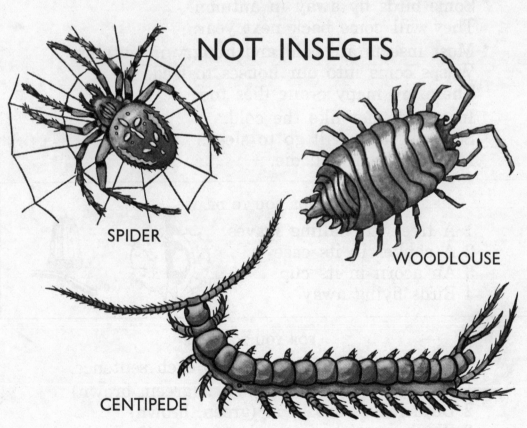

SPIDER

WOODLOUSE

CENTIPEDE

THE SEASON WHICH FOLLOWS SUMMER

* In summer the weather is hot.
In winter it is cold.
* AUTUMN is the beginning of winter.
* We put on extra clothes in autumn.
* It becomes dark earlier.
* Sometimes we have mist.
* When leaves are green, they are alive.
Leaves turn brown when they die.
* There are brown leaves on many plants in autumn.
Brown leaves fall off the trees in autumn.
* We find horse chestnuts, and we find acorns.
* Some birds fly away in autumn.
They will come back next year.
* Most insects are cold and hungry in autumn.
Wasps come into our houses to feed.
There are many crane flies too.
* Insects do not like the cold.
Some of them will go to sleep.
Many of them will die.

FOR YOU TO DRAW

1 A tree with falling leaves
2 A conker in its case
3 An acorn in its cup
4 Birds flying away

FOR YOU TO WRITE

Put the right word into each sentence.

1 Most living leaves are . . . . . (green, brown)
2 Dead leaves are . . . . . (green, brown)
3 Wasps come to jam pots to . . . . . (feed, sleep)
4 Some . . . . . fly away. (mammals, birds)

AUTUMN

THE DAYS GET COLDER   **SOME LEAVES TURN BROWN**

HORSE CHESTNUT   OAK ACORN

LEAVES, CHESTNUTS AND ACORNS FALL OFF THE TREES

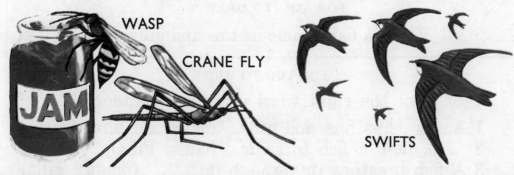

WASP

CRANE FLY

SWIFTS

INSECTS COME IN TO KEEP WARM   **SOME BIRDS FLY AWAY**

FOR YOU TO DO

1 Collect dead leaves for your science table.
2 Collect other things which fall from trees. Try to find the trees they come from.
3 Look for different toadstools.
4 Find out the names of any insects in your house.
5 Watch for birds flying away.

ANIMALS WITH FINS AND GILLS

* All fish have fins.
The fins of a fish help it to swim.
* All fish have gills.
The gills of a fish help it to breathe under water.
* A fish breathes in through its mouth.
It breathes out through its gills.
* A fish is an animal with fins and gills.
* Most fish have scales on their bodies.
Some fish do not have scales.
The catfish and the dogfish have no scales.
* Some fish live in fresh water.
The goldfish and the stickleback live in fresh water.
* Some fish live in the sea.
The plaice and the flying fish live in the sea.
The flying fish cannot really fly. It can only glide.

FOR YOU TO DRAW

Draw a fish. Name its fins and gills.

FOR YOU TO WRITE

Put the right word into each sentence.

1 A . . . . . has fins and gills. (mammal, bird, fish)
2 . . . . . help a fish to swim. (Gills, Fins)
3 A fish breathes in through its . . . . . (mouth, gills)
4 A fish breathes out through its . . . . . (mouth, gills)
5 A . . . . . has no scales. (goldfish, catfish)

FOR YOU TO DO

1 Watch a fish breathe in through its mouth.
2 Watch it breathe out through its gills.
3 Put your hands to your head and pretend they are gills.
Open your mouth, and close your gills.
Close your mouth, and open your gills.
4 Count how many fins of each kind there are on a fish.

FISH
FRESH WATER

GOLDFISH

STICKLEBACKS

CATFISH

SOME FISH LIVE IN FRESH WATER

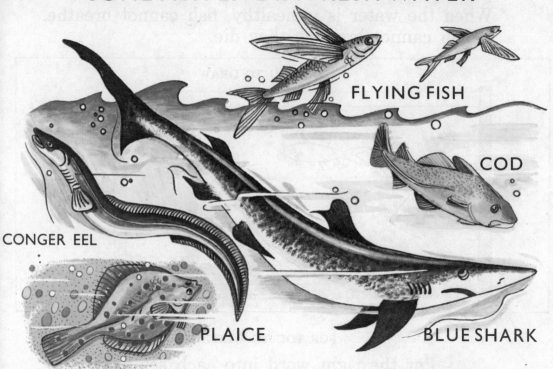

FLYING FISH

COD

CONGER EEL

PLAICE

BLUE SHARK

SOME FISH LIVE IN SEA WATER

THE FINS AND GILLS OF A DOGFISH

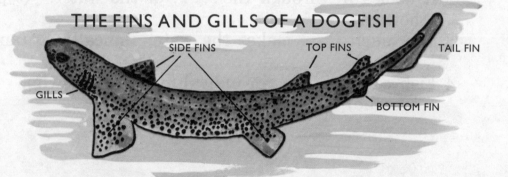

SIDE FINS

TOP FINS

TAIL FIN

GILLS

BOTTOM FIN

TAKING CARE OF FISH

* A fish must breathe.
  If it cannot breathe, it dies.

* Fresh air comes to us through an open window.
  The top of the water is the window to the fish.
  The fresh air goes in very slowly.
  It needs to be a big window.

* Fish must have food.
  They do not like too much food.
  Too much food makes the water unhealthy.

* When the water is unhealthy, fish cannot breathe.
  If fish cannot breathe, they die.

FOR YOU TO DRAW

A

HAPPY

HOME

FOR YOU TO WRITE

Put the right word into each sentence.

1 Fish need . . . . . air. (fresh, used)

2 It comes in through the . . . . . of the water. (top, bottom)

3 Too much . . . . . makes the water unhealthy. (air, food)

4 Fish cannot . . . . . in unhealthy water. (swim, breathe)

UNHAPPY HOMES

AN AQUARIUM

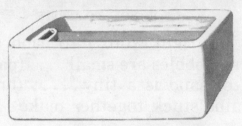

AN OLD SINK

HAPPY HOMES

FOR YOU TO DO

1 Look for fish which are gasping at the top of the water. These are fish that are short of fresh air.
2 If you keep fish, see that there is plenty of room for fresh air at the top of the water.

NEVER-ALIVE THINGS ON THE EARTH

* Rock is never-alive.
* Boulders are big pieces of rock.
* Pebbles and stones are small pieces of rock.
* Very tiny pebbles and stones are called grains.
* We sometimes find millions of grains of certain rocks. We call this SAND.
* Sometimes millions of grains of sand are stuck together. We call this SANDSTONE.
* Very small grains of rock form a powder. Some kinds of rock powder will mix with water to form a paste. We call this paste CLAY.
* Bricks and pots are made of clay which has been baked.

FOR YOU TO DRAW

1 Draw a picture of huge rocks and tiny rocks.
2 Draw something made from rock.

FOR YOU TO WRITE

Put the right word into each sentence.
1 Stones and pebbles are small . . . . (paste, rocks)
2 A grain of sand is a tiny . . . . . (brick, pebble)
3 Sand grains stuck together make . . . . . (sandstone, clay)
4 Pots are made of baked . . . . . (sandstone, clay)

FOR YOU TO DO

1 Collect some different things which are rock.
2 Collect different colours of sand, pebbles and stones.
3 Rub two pieces of sandstone together and collect the grains of sand.
4 Let a piece of clay dry. See how it changes.

ROCKS

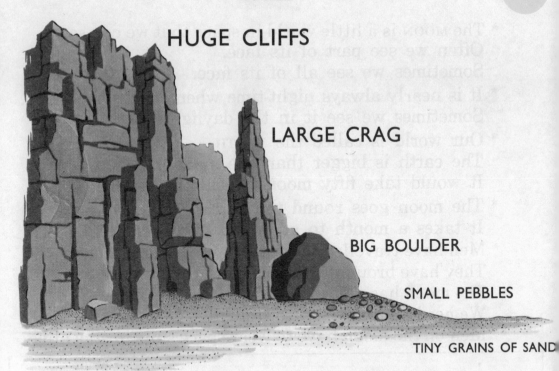

HUGE CLIFFS

LARGE CRAG

BIG BOULDER

SMALL PEBBLES

TINY GRAINS OF SAND

HUGE ROCKS TO TINY ROCKS

PEBBLE   SANDSTONE   CLAY   BASALT   SLATE

THINGS MADE FROM BAKED CLAY

* The MOON is a little world in space that we can see.
Often we see part of its face.
Sometimes we see all of its face.
* It is nearly always night-time when we see the moon.
Sometimes we see it in the daylight.
* Our world is called the EARTH.
The earth is bigger than the moon.
It would take fifty moons to fill the earth.
* The moon goes round the earth.
It takes a month to go round once.
* Men have travelled to the moon in space vehicles.
They have brought back pieces of rock from the moon.
The moon has no air. It has very little water.
We need air and water to stay alive.
Men on the moon have to wear space suits to stay alive.

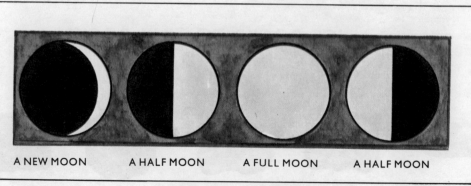

A NEW MOON   A HALF MOON   A FULL MOON   A HALF MOON

FOR YOU TO WRITE

Put the right words in the right places.

1 The . . . . . goes round the . . . . . (earth, moon)
2 It takes a . . . . . to go round once. (day, week, month)
3 The . . . . . is smaller than the . . . . . (earth, moon)
4 . . . . . moons would fill the earth. (Two, Ten, Fifty)

FOR YOU TO DO

1 Look at a tennis ball and a glass marble to see the
   different sizes of the earth and the moon.
2 Look for the different shapes that the moon shows.

EARTH AND MOON

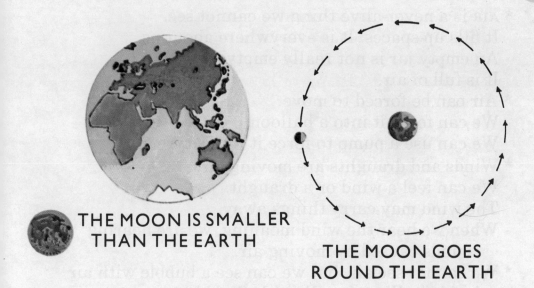

THE MOON IS SMALLER
THAN THE EARTH

THE MOON GOES
ROUND THE EARTH

MEN ON THE MOON

NEVER-ALIVE THINGS ON THE EARTH

* AIR is a never-alive thing we cannot see.
  It fills up spaces. It is everywhere about us.
  An empty jar is not really empty.
  It is full of air.
* Air can be forced to move.
  We can force it into a balloon.
  We can use a pump to force it into a tyre.
* Winds and draughts are moving air.
  We can feel a wind or a draught.
  The wind may carry things away.
  When we hear the wind moaning, we are hearing
      sounds caused by moving air.
* We cannot see air, but we can see a bubble with air
      inside it. We can collect the bubbles.
* We need air; we breathe air; we use air.
  Without it we would die.

FOR YOU TO DRAW

1 A bottle full of air
2 A windy day

FOR YOU TO WRITE

1 Air fills up . . . . . (water, spaces)
2 . . . . . are moving air. (Winds, Balloons)
3 We can . . . . . the wind. (see, feel)
4 . . . . . can be collected. (Bubbles, Air)

FOR YOU TO DO

1 Experiment with air in a sink full of water.
2 Find some ways of forcing air to move.
3 If there is a draught find out where it comes from.
4 Collect some things with air spaces in them.

AIR IS SOMETHING

WATER CANNOT GO IN UNTIL AIR CAN GO OUT

AIR CAN BE FORCED TO MOVE

WINDS AND DRAUGHTS ARE MOVING AIR

WATER CANNOT COME OUT UNTIL AIR CAN GO IN

COLLECTING BUBBLES OF AIR

LIVING THINGS IN WINTER

* WINTER is the coldest part of the year.
* If living things become too cold they die.
  Animals meet the winter in different ways.
* Some birds fly away to warmer lands.
  Some birds stay and grow more feathers.
  They fluff out their feathers to keep themselves warm.
* Pond fish rest when the water is cold.
  They eat a lot of food in autumn.
  They may not eat at all in winter.
  They will rest until they feel the warmth of spring.
* Many insects die in autumn.
  Many sleep all through the winter.
  If there is frost, some of them die.
* Some mammals grow longer hair in autumn.
  They grow it to keep themselves warm in winter.
  Some mammals sleep through the coldness of winter.
  They will sleep until the warmer weather of spring.

FOR YOU TO DRAW

1 A robin with fluffed-out feathers
2 A fish at rest beneath the ice
3 A queen bumble bee asleep in a hole

FOR YOU TO WRITE

Put these words into the right sentences:
mammals, Feathers, rest, cold, frost, Hair

1 If animals become too ..... they die.
2 Some ..... sleep until the spring.
3 Fish ..... throughout the winter.
4 ..... help to keep birds warm.
5 ..... helps to keep mammals warm.
6 Some insects are killed by the .....

THE ANIMALS

BIRDS FLUFF OUT THEIR
FEATHERS TO KEEP WARM

FISH REST BENEATH THE ICE

MANY INSECTS DIE

SOME INSECTS SLEEP

SOME MAMMALS GROW MORE HAIR

SOME MAMMALS SLEEP

FOR YOU TO DO

1 Put out some bread and seeds for the birds.
  Put out a saucer of water as well.
2 Look for feeding birds with fluffed-out feathers.
3 Look for insects in their winter sleep.
  Do not disturb them if you find them.
4 Look for mammals with thick fur.

LIVING THINGS IN WINTER

* Most plants rest in winter.
Some plants die.
* Some plants keep all their leaves in winter.
Some plants lose a few.
Some plants lose them all.
* Most plants need sunshine to grow.
They do not get a lot in winter.
We do not mow the lawn or cut hedges.
* The holly loses some of its leaves in winter.
It keeps the rest.
We hang its branches in our homes at Christmas.
* The spruce fir likes the cold.
We hang our presents on it at Christmas.
* The mistletoe plant has pale green leaves.
We have a special use for that at Christmas.
* Plants which lose their leaves look sad and bare.
They will grow new leaves in spring.

FOR YOU TO DRAW

HOLLY   MISTLETOE

ROSE
PLANT

Some plants keep
green leaves.

Some plants have
lost their leaves.

FOR YOU TO WRITE

Put these words into the right sentences:
Christmas, die, oak tree, rest

1 Most plants . . . . . in winter.
2 Some plants . . . . . in winter.
3 The . . . . . does not stay green in winter.
4 We use the spruce fir for a . . . . . tree.

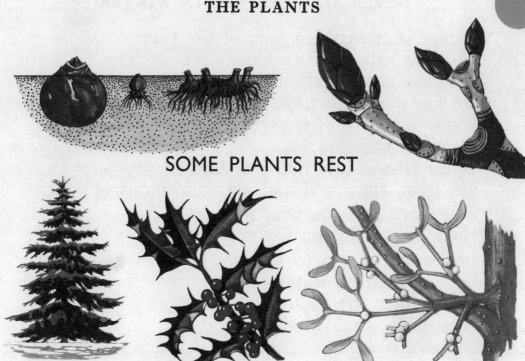

SOME PLANTS REST

SOME PLANTS STAY GREEN

| ASH | OAK | BIRCH | POPLAR |

SOME PLANTS HAVE NO LEAVES LEFT

FOR YOU TO DO

1 Look for plants which have died.
2 Look for plants which have kept their leaves.
3 Look for living plants which have lost their leaves.

NEVER-ALIVE THINGS IN WINTER

* Winter is the coldest part of the year.
  We have rain, and we have sleet.
  We have snow, and we have frost.
  We may sometimes have hail.
* Water freezes into frost.
  Water freezes into ice.
  Water freezes into hail and into snow.
  Ice, frost, snow and hail are solid forms of water.
* Frost forms on the window pane.
  Hoar frost forms on the ground.
* Icicles are formed by dripping water.
* Ice will float on water.
  It is lighter than water.
  It is colder than water.

FOR YOU TO DRAW

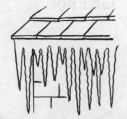

Ice is solid water.

Ice floats in water.

FOR YOU TO WRITE

Put these words into the right sentences:
water, freezes, float, ground, warmed

1 Water ..... when it is cold enough.
2 Snow and frost are solid forms of .....
3 Hoar frost forms on the .....
4 Ice will ..... on water.
5 When ice and snow are ....., they turn back into
  water.

FROST ON
A WINDOW

FALLING
SNOW

ICICLES FROM A BURST PIPE

ICE ON A POND

SNOW

A CRACKED JAR

FOR YOU TO DO

1 Feel which side of the window pane the frost is on.
2 Look at the patterns the frost has made.
3 Look for hoar frost on the ground.
4 Look for snowclouds in the sky.
5 Leave a jar of water outside at night. See if the
   ice will break it.

* The STARS are hot and glowing.
  Our sun is hot and glowing.
  The sun is a star.
* The stars are there all the time.
  We do not see them in daylight.
  The sun outshines them.
* The earth goes round the sun.
  It takes one year to go round once.
* The sun is much bigger than the earth.
  The sun seems smaller because it is so far away.
* Some of the stars are smaller than the sun.
  Some of the stars are bigger than the sun.
  They all seem smaller than the sun.
  They are so very, very far away.

FOR YOU TO DRAW

The sun is bigger
than the earth.   EARTH ⊕

FOR YOU TO WRITE

Put these words into the right sentences:
bigger, earth, sun, stars, year

1 The . . . . . is a star.
2 The . . . . . goes round the sun.
3 It goes round once a . . . . .
4 The sun is . . . . . than the earth.
5 Some . . . . . are bigger than the sun.

FOR YOU TO DO

1 Watch the stars twinkle at night.
2 See if you can find one which does not twinkle.
3 Find out about other things which go round the sun.

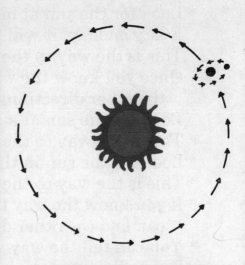

THE SUN IS A STAR LIKE THESE

THE EARTH GOES ROUND THE SUN

THE SUN IS MUCH BIGGER

FINDING THE WAY

* There are four main ways you can go.
  They are NORTH, SOUTH, EAST and WEST.
  You can tell the way by looking at the sun.
* Look for the sun at midday.
  Every midday, it will be in the same direction.
  This is the way to the south.
  Once you know the way to the south, you can find
    the other directions.
  Look for the sun at sunset.
  This is the way to the west.
* Look for the sun in the early morning.
  This is the way to the east.
* If you know the way to the west, or to the east, you
    can find the other directions.
* You can tell the way with a magnetic compass.
  Its needle always points in the same direction.
  One end always points to the north.
  The other end always points to the south.
* The end which points to the north may have 'N' on it.
* If you know your way to the north, you can find the
    other directions.

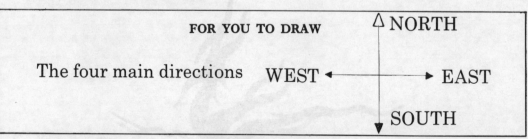

FOR YOU TO DRAW

The four main directions

NORTH
WEST ← → EAST
SOUTH

FOR YOU TO WRITE

Put these words into the right sentences :
north, south, east, west

1 The sun seems to rise in the . . . . .
2 The sun is to the . . . . . at midday.
3 The sun is to the . . . . . at sunset.
4 A compass needle points . . . . . and south.

NORTH, SOUTH, EAST, WEST

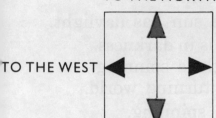

TO THE NORTH

TO THE WEST — TO THE EAST

TO THE SOUTH

SOUTH IS WHERE YOU SEE THE SUN AT MID-DAY

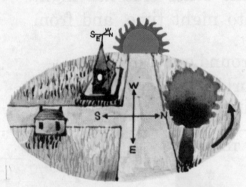

WEST IS WHERE YOU SEE THE SUN AT SUNSET

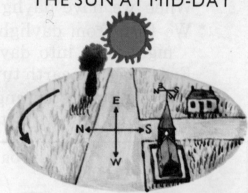

EAST IS WHERE YOU SEE THE SUN AT SUNRISE

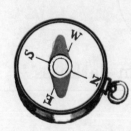

A MAGNETIC COMPASS

FOR YOU TO DO

1 Find out which are the four ways from your school.
2 Find out which are the four ways from your home.
3 Ask to be shown how to use a magnetic compass.

DAY AND NIGHT

* You cannot see our sun at night.
  It is at the other side of the earth.
* The side of the earth facing the sun has daylight.
  The side that faces the other way is in darkness.
* As you work and play, our earth is spinning.
  You ride through the day on a turning world.
* As you sleep, the earth goes on spinning.
  You ride through the night on a turning world.
* When we are in darkness the other side of the earth is
  in daylight.
  When we have daylight, the other side has night.
* We turn from daylight into night time, and from
  night time into daylight.
  Every day the earth turns round once.
* We live on a spinning world.
  The earth is always turning.

FOR YOU TO DRAW

My house in daylight   My house in darkness

FOR YOU TO WRITE

Put these words into the right sentences:
spins, daylight, day, darkness

1 We have night and day because the earth.....
2 The earth takes a..... to turn round once.
3 When we have night, the other side has.....
4 When we have daylight, the other side has.....

FOR YOU TO DO

1 Mark where a patch of sunlight falls on the floor or on the board. Look for the same patch later.
2 Find the sunrise and sunset sides of your room.

THE TWO KINDS OF DEAD THINGS

* The two kinds of living things are animals and plants.
The two kinds of dead things are animals and plants.
Most dead things are only parts of animals or plants.
* Some dead things are parts from living animals or
   plants.
Wool and feathers may come from living animals.
A piece of tree bark may come from a living plant.
These are all dead parts from living things.
* Some dead things are parts of dead animals or plants.
Frozen meat and frozen fish come from dead animals.
Wood and pickled onions come from dead plants.
These are all dead parts from dead things.
* Some of the things we use are made from dead parts.
A woollen scarf and a fur coat are made from dead
   animal parts. They are dead animal things.
Cotton cloth, linen cloth, and string are made from
   dead plant parts. Some paper is made from wood.
Cotton, linen, paper and string are dead plant things.
* When animal and plant parts are cooked, they are dead.
Boiled ham and roast chicken are dead animal things.
Potatoes and carrots are living plant parts.
After they are cooked, they are dead plant parts.

FOR YOU TO DRAW

Some dead animal things and dead plant things.

FOR YOU TO WRITE

Put these words into the right sentences:
animal, plants, made, two, dead

1 The . . . . . kinds of dead things are animals and plants.
2 Wool and feather are dead . . . . . things.
3 Frozen meat and pickled onions are . . . . . things.
4 Some of the things we use are . . . . . from dead parts.
5 Cooked animals and . . . . . are dead.

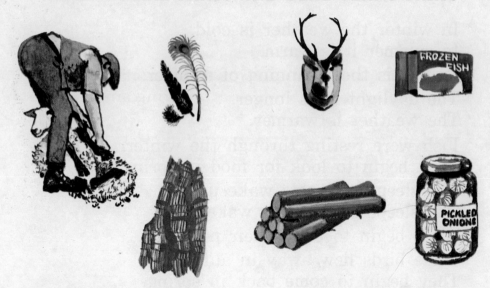

DEAD PARTS FROM
LIVING THINGS

DEAD PARTS FROM
DEAD THINGS

THINGS MADE FROM DEAD PARTS

COOKED FOODS
ARE DEAD

FOR YOU TO DO

1 When you have a meal, find out which parts are plant and which are animal.
2 Of the clothes you wear, try to find out which are dead animal and which are dead plant.

THE SEASON WHICH FOLLOWS WINTER

* In winter the weather is cold.
  In summer it is warm.
* SPRING is the beginning of summer.
* The daylight lasts longer.
  The weather is warmer.
* Fish were resting through the winter.
  They begin to look for food in spring.
* The sleeping insects wake up.
  The sleeping mammals wake up.
* Birds begin to build their nests.
* Some birds flew away in autumn.
  They begin to come back in spring.
* Many plants begin to grow.
  Buds open on the trees.
  Some plants have flowers.
* Spring is the end of winter.
  Spring is the season of awakening.

FOR YOU TO DRAW

1 Spring flowers
2 Birds returning

FOR YOU TO WRITE

Put these words into the right sentences:
awaken, grow, nests, born, return, food

1 Baby plants begin to . . . . . in spring.
2 Many baby animals are . . . . . in spring.
3 Sleeping animals . . . . . in spring.
4 Fish find more . . . . . in spring.
5 Some birds build . . . . . in spring.
6 Some birds . . . . . in spring.

SPRING

THE DAYS GET WARMER

BIRDS RETURN

INSECTS WAKE UP

MAMMALS WAKE UP

PLANTS BEGIN TO GROW

BUDS OPEN ON THE TREES

FOR YOU TO DO

1 Look for baby plants beginning to grow.
2 Look for insects. Count their legs.
3 Watch for birds returning.
4 Find a bird's nest. Look at it. DO NOT TOUCH.

51

PLANT PARTS TO LOOK FOR

* There are two main kinds of plants in the world.
* Some are simple plants.
* The rest have roots, stems and leaves.
* The roots hold the plant in the soil.
  They take in food and water.
  When the roots can feed, the plant can grow.
* The stem grows up from the roots.
  It takes the food and water to the leaves.
  It lifts the leaves into the sunlight.
  It lifts them into the air.
* Leaves grow from the stem.
  They are nearly always green.
  They take in the sunlight. They take in the air.
* Most land plants have roots, a stem and leaves.
  Some fresh-water plants have roots, a stem and leaves.
  The simple seaweeds do not have these parts.

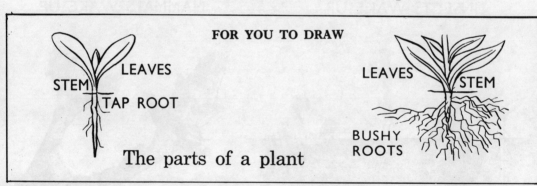

FOR YOU TO DRAW

LEAVES
STEM
TAP ROOT

The parts of a plant

LEAVES
STEM
BUSHY ROOTS

FOR YOU TO WRITE

Put these words into the right sentences:
Roots, stem, Leaves, Many, water

1 . . . . . plants have roots, a stem and leaves.
2 . . . . . hold the plants in the soil.
3 The roots take in . . . . .
4 The . . . . . takes the water to the leaves.
5 . . . . . take in sunlight and air.

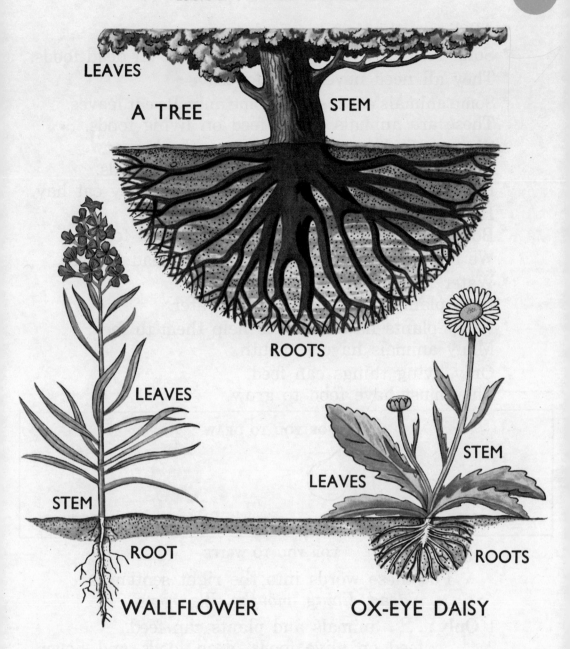

LEAVES

A TREE

STEM

ROOTS

LEAVES

STEM

ROOT

WALLFLOWER

LEAVES

STEM

ROOTS

OX-EYE DAISY

FOR YOU TO DO

1 Grow a carrot top in a saucer of water.
2 Look for roots, stem and leaves on a plant.
3 Collect different leaves for your notebook.

53

* All living things must feed.

* Some feed on living foods. Some feed on dead foods.

* They all need never-alive foods.

* Some animals eat insects. Some animals eat leaves.
These are animals which feed on living foods.

* We may find maggots feeding on dead meat.
These are animals which feed on dead foods.

* In summer horses eat grass. In winter they eat hay.
Horses eat alive foods and dead foods.

* Boiled eggs and fish and chips are dead foods.
We are animals who eat living and dead foods.

* Water is a never-alive food.
Both plants and animals need water.

* Many plants have roots to help them to feed.
Many animals have a mouth.

* Only living things can feed.
They must have food to grow.

FOR YOU TO DRAW

Some alive foods

Some dead foods

FOR YOU TO WRITE

Put these words into the right sentences :
~~dead~~, ~~living~~, mouths, ~~We~~, ~~roots~~

1 Only ..... animals and plants can feed.
2 ..... feed on alive foods, dead foods and never-alive foods.
3 Cooked foods are ..... foods.
4 Many plants feed through their .....
5 Many animals feed through their .....

LIVING THINGS FEED

SOME ANIMALS EAT ALIVE FOODS

SOME ANIMALS EAT DEAD FOODS

PLANTS AND ANIMALS NEED NEVER-ALIVE FOODS

FOR YOU TO DO

When you have a meal, try to find out which of your foods are alive, which are dead, and which are 'never alive'.

55

* Living things GROW.

Dead things do not grow.

Never-alive things do not grow.

* A wooden ruler is dead. It will not grow.

* A pebble is never-alive. It will not grow.

* Only living things grow.

* Children begin life as babies.

When they have grown up they are adults.

* Young animals and plants feed.

They feed to help them grow.

They grow into adults.

* Some adult animals stop growing.

* Other adult animals and plants go on growing.

When they stop feeding, they stop growing.

When they are dead, they stop growing.

FOR YOU TO DRAW

Living things grow up.

FOR YOU TO WRITE

Put these words into the right sentences :

~~food~~, ~~growing~~, ~~living~~, animals, ~~adults~~

1 All . . . . . things grow.

2 They need . . . . . to grow.

3 Young animals and plants grow into . . . . .

4 Adult plants go on . . . . .

5 Some adult . . . . . stop growing.

MAMMALS

FISH

BIRDS

INSECTS

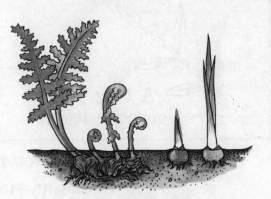

PLANTS

FOR YOU TO DO

1 Find out how tall you are.
2 Find out how heavy you are.

26

STEMS AND LEAVES

* Trees that have no green leaves in winter are called
  DECIDUOUS.
* Deciduous trees lose their leaves in autumn.
  They grow new leaves in spring.
  Twigs with new leaves grow from buds on the stem.
  A twig is only another length of stem.
* On some trees the leaves grow from the twig in twos.
  We say that these leaves are OPPOSITE on the stem.
* On some trees the leaves grow in ones on the stem.
  We say that these leaves are ALTERNATE on the stem.
* Horse chestnut leaves grow from the twig in twos.
  Sycamore leaves grow from the twig in twos.
  Horse chestnut and sycamore leaves
    are opposite leaves.
* Beech leaves grow from the twig in ones.
  Oak leaves grow from the twig in ones.
  Beech leaves and oak leaves are alternate leaves.

FOR YOU TO DRAW

A twig with
opposite leaves

A twig with
alternate leaves

FOR YOU TO WRITE

Fill in the missing words yourself.
1 Twigs with new leaves grow from . . . . . on the stem.
2 Alternate leaves grow from the twig in . . . . .
3 Opposite leaves grow from the twig in . . . . .
4 Oak leaves are . . . . . leaves.
5 Horse chestnut leaves are . . . . . leaves.

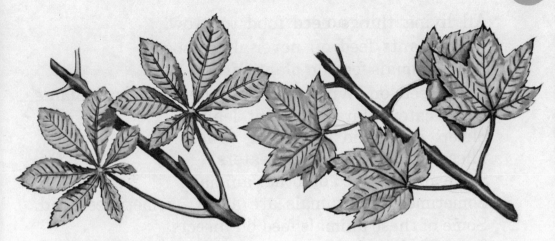

HORSE CHESTNUT   SYCAMORE

THESE LEAVES ARE OPPOSITE ON THE STEM

BEECH   OAK

THESE LEAVES ARE ALTERNATE ON THE STEM

FOR YOU TO DO

1 Look for stems with opposite leaves.
  Look for stems with alternate leaves.
2 Peel a bud to see what is inside.
3 See if you can find a bud
  from which a flower is growing.

27

WHAT ANIMALS FEED ON

* All living things need food to grow.
* Most plants feed on never-alive foods.
* Some animals feed on plant parts.
  Some feed on living plants; others on dead plants.
* Some caterpillars eat plant leaves.
  Sheep, cows and horses eat grass.
  These animals are plant-eaters.
* Some animals feed on other animals.
  Sometimes the animals are alive; sometimes dead.
  Some of these animals feed on insects.
  Some birds eat fish.
  Lions and tigers eat large animals.
  Some fish eat smaller fish.
  These animals are animal-eaters.
* The crow eats both animal foods and plant foods.
  We eat both animal foods and plant foods.

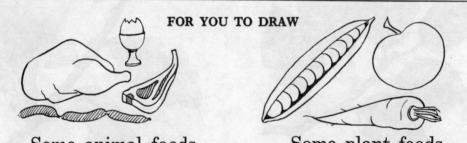

FOR YOU TO DRAW

Some animal foods   Some plant foods

FOR YOU TO WRITE

Fill in the missing words yourself.

1 All living things need food to . . . .
2 Most plants feed on . . . . . foods.
3 Some animals . . . . . on plant parts.
4 Some animals feed on other . . . . .
5 Some animals feed on other . . . . . and on . . . . .

PLANT FOODS AND ANIMAL FOODS

SOME ANIMALS EAT PLANTS

SOME ANIMALS EAT OTHER ANIMALS

SOME ANIMALS EAT BOTH

FOR YOU TO DO

1 Of the foods you eat, find out which are animal and which are plant.

2 Find out what kinds of food the zoo animals eat.

3 Find out what kinds of food your pet eats.

28

LIVING PLANTS IN SUMMER

* Green plants like the summer.
  They grow best in sunlight.
* Many of them have roots, stems and leaves.
  Their roots and stems grow longer.
  They grow more leaves as well.
* Many of them grow flowers. Some do not.
* The buttercup plant grows yellow flowers.
  The dandelion plant grows golden flowers.
  The flowers of the daisy are yellow and white.
* The horse chestnut tree grows flowers in early summer.
  The flowers grow in clusters that look like candles.
* These four plants have roots, stems and leaves.
  They are also plants that have flowers.
* Not all plants have flowers.
  Not all plants have roots, stems and leaves.
  Some are not even green.

FOR YOU TO DRAW

HORSE CHESTNUT   DAISY   BUTTERCUP   DANDELION

FOR YOU TO WRITE

Fill in the missing words yourself.

1 Green . . . . . grow best in sunlight.
2 Buttercup flowers are . . . . . in colour.
3 The flowers of the daisy are yellow and . . . . .
4 Dandelion flowers are . . . . .
5 Horse chestnut trees grow . . . . . in early summer.
6 Horse chestnut flowers look like . . . . .

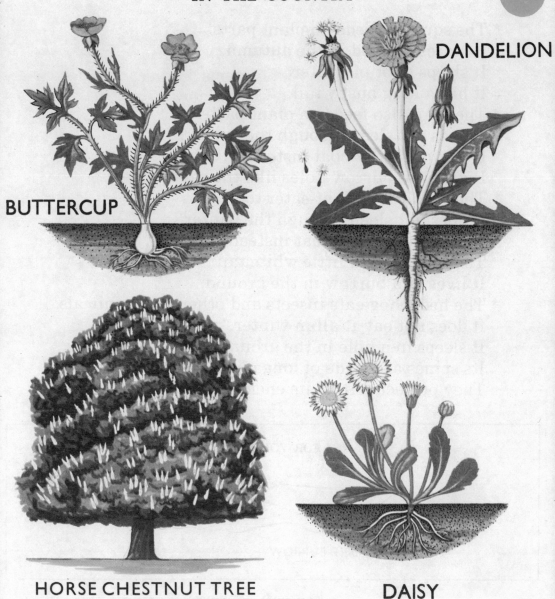

BUTTERCUP

DANDELION

HORSE CHESTNUT TREE
WITH FLOWERS

DAISY

FOR YOU TO DO

1 Look for the roots, stem and leaves of plants.
2 Find a dandelion flower. Look to see what has
   happened to it in a day or two.
3 Gather wild flowers and stand them in pots of water.

⋆ The squirrel feeds on plant parts.
It stores its food in the autumn.
It sleeps a lot in winter.
It has a long bushy tail.
⋆ The hare also feeds on plant parts.
It does not sleep through the winter.
It grows a paler coat instead.
It does not burrow holes like the rabbit does.
⋆ The rabbit is a plant-eater too.
It does not sleep through the winter.
It grows a thicker coat instead.
The rabbit has a little white tail.
It lives in a burrow in the ground.
⋆ The hedgehog eats insects and other small animals.
It does not eat at all in winter.
It sleeps in a hole in the ground.
Its spines are made of long stiff hairs.
They protect it from its enemies.

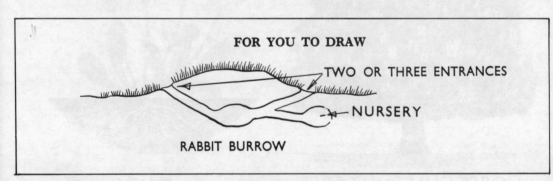

FOR YOU TO DRAW

TWO OR THREE ENTRANCES

NURSERY

RABBIT BURROW

FOR YOU TO WRITE

Fill in the missing words yourself.

1 The hedgehog is an . . . . .-eater.
2 The squirrel eats parts of . . . . .
3 The rabbit is a . . . . .-eater.
4 The hare is a . . . . .-eater.
5 The hedgehog . . . . . through the winter.

IN THE COUNTRY

GREY SQUIRREL
IN HIS DREY

BLACK TIPS ON EARS

HARE

NO BLACK TIPS

HEDGEHOG

WILD RABBIT

FOR YOU TO DO

1 See which of these mammals have their eyes in the
   side of their head and which have them in front.
2 If you know someone with a pet rabbit, find out
   what kind of food it eats. Try to see its teeth.

* A young insect is called a LARVA.
* The water beetle larva feeds on other animals.
  So does the water beetle adult.
  The larva sleeps through the winter.
  It sleeps in a hole above the water.
  Both larva and adult breathe at the top of the water.
* The bluebottle larva feeds on dead mammals, dead
  birds and dead fish. So does the adult.
  The larva has no legs. The adult has only two wings.
* The mother bumble bee sleeps through the winter.
  In the spring she builds a nest.
  She gathers food from flowers for her babies.
  She feeds on food from flowers herself.
* The garden tiger moth has pretty colours.
  The larva feeds on plant leaves.
  It is called a caterpillar. It has six legs.
  It also has stumps to help its tail along.
  The stumps are not legs.

FOR YOU TO DRAW

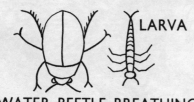
LARVA

WATER BEETLE BREATHING   CATERPILLAR FEEDING

FOR YOU TO WRITE

Fill in the missing words yourself.

1 Some water beetles feed on other living . . . . .
2 Water beetles come to the top of the water to . . . . .
3 Bluebottles feed on dead . . . . .
4 The . . . . . feeds its young.
5 The garden tiger larva feeds on . . . . .

WATER BEETLE AND LARVA   HOW MANY WINGS?   **BLUEBOTTLE AND LARVA**

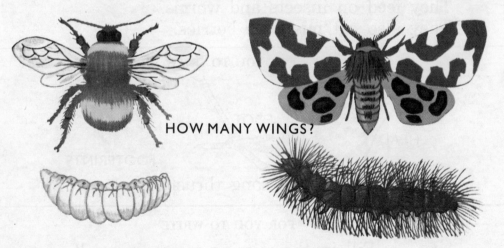

HOW MANY WINGS?

BUMBLE BEE AND LARVA   **GARDEN TIGER AND LARVA**

FOR YOU TO DO

Look at the legs of a caterpillar.
Look at the stumps that help its tail along.
See how they differ from its true legs.

* The swallow feeds on living insects.
It catches them when they are flying.
There are no insects for its food in winter.
The swallow flies away to find some.
It comes back in the spring.

* The barn owl stays through the winter.
It feeds on mammals and small birds.
It rests during the daylight.
It hunts for its food at night.

* The wood pigeon stays through the winter.
It feeds on grain and acorns and berries.
It sometimes eats caterpillars.

* Some thrushes fly away for the winter.
They come back in the spring.
Some of them stay here all the time.
They feed on insects and worms.
They also eat mistletoe berries.

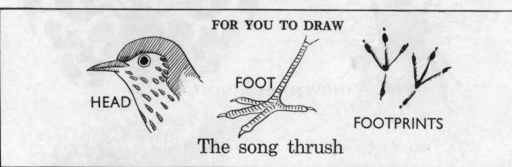

FOR YOU TO DRAW

HEAD FOOT FOOTPRINTS

The song thrush

FOR YOU TO WRITE

Fill in the missing words yourself.

1 All the . . . . . fly away in the autumn.

2 They have no . . . . . to feed on.

3 The barn owl eats both mammals and . . . . .

4 The . . . . . likes acorns.

5 The . . . . . hunts at night.

6 The thrush eats . . . . . and . . . . . foods.

SWALLOW

BARN OWL

WOOD PIGEON

SONG THRUSH

FOR YOU TO DO

1 Watch for several swallows flying together.
2 Listen for the call of an owl at night.
3 Watch birds collecting for their nests.
4 Watch birds to find out what they feed on.
5 Look in the trees for a bird's nest. Do not
  disturb it.

32

LIVING FISH IN SUMMER

* Most fish feed on animal foods.
* Sticklebacks live in ponds and lakes.
  They feed on insects and other small animals.
  The father stickleback has a red breast in summer.
  He builds a nest amongst the plants.
  Baby sticklebacks hatch out in the nest.
  The father stickleback looks after them.
* Minnows live in streams and rivers.
  They swim together in a crowd.
  A crowd of fish is called a shoal.
  Minnows feed on insects and worms.
  They also feed on water plants.
* The trout lives in streams and rivers and lakes.
  It has spots on its sides.
  The trout feeds on sticklebacks and minnows.
  It also eats other water animals.
* The pike lives in lakes and rivers.
  It feeds on birds and mammals and other fish.
  The pike has teeth.
  It is a greedy fish.

FOR YOU TO DRAW

I A TROUT   2 A PIKE

FOR YOU TO WRITE

Fill in the missing words yourself.

1 Most fish feed on . . . . . foods.
2 Father stickleback has a . . . . . breast in summer.
3 The . . . . . is a greedy fish.
4 . . . . . swim together in shoals.
5 The . . . . . has spots on its sides.
6 It feeds on other . . . . .

STICKLEBACK

TROUT

MINNOW

PIKE

FOR YOU TO DO

1 Look for the three spines on a stickleback.
 Look for the red breast of the father stickleback.
 Look for the silver breast of the female fish.
2 Count the fins of any fish, if you can see them.
 Look for single fins, and for fins in pairs.
3 If you keep fish, remember:
   a) you should keep them in happy homes – not in jam
   jars or goldfish bowls.
   b) you must not keep too many fish together.

33

NEVER-ALIVE THINGS IN SUMMER

* Rocks, pebbles and sand are never-alive.
* The waves of the sea are caused by the wind.
  The sea is never-alive.
* The clouds in the sky are moved by the wind.
  Rain falls from the clouds.
  Rain and clouds are never-alive.
* The wind itself is never-alive.
* Empty shells that we find on the shore are never-alive.
  They were the homes of the animals which built them.
  The animals which built them were alive.
  Sea birds and other animals ate them.
  They did not eat the shells.
  The shells are never-alive.
* We may find cockle and mussel shells tightly closed.
  Then perhaps the animals are still alive inside them.
* We seldom find the razor shell closed up.
  We seldom find a whelk shell on the sand with the
    animal inside it.
* Cockle, mussel and razor shells have two parts.
  The whelk shell has only one.

FOR YOU TO DRAW

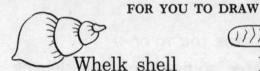 Whelk shell   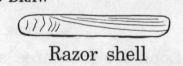 Razor shell

---

FOR YOU TO WRITE

Fill in the missing words yourself.

1 The . . . . . moves the clouds.
2 We get . . . . . from the clouds.
3 Cockle and mussel shells are in . . . . . parts.
4 The . . . . . shell is in one part.
5 . . . . . ate the animals that built the shells.

CLOUDS

ROCK

SEA

SAND

WHELK SHELL

MUSSEL
SHELL

COCKLE SHELL

RAZOR
SHELL

FOR YOU TO DO

1 Collect sands and pebbles of different colours.
2 Collect seashells of different shapes.
  Find out whether they should be in one or two
    parts.
3 Find whether the breeze is blowing in from the sea,
    or out to the sea, during the daytime.

34

* Many plants grow in the sea.
Only a few kinds grow in sand.

* Marram grass is a land plant.
It grows in the sandhills along the shore.
Its leaves are thin and spiky.
Its roots and stems stop the wind from blowing the
sand away.

* The sea pink is a land plant.
It grows on the rocks and cliffs above the sea.
It is a plant we can grow in the garden.
In summer it has pink flowers.

* Sea plants have no roots, stems, or leaves.
Sometimes they look as though they have.
Sea plants have no flowers either.
Sea plants are called seaweeds.

* The green sea lettuce is a green sea plant.
It can be made into a jelly and used for food.

* The bladderwrack is a brown sea plant.
It has bladders which help it to float.

FOR YOU TO DRAW

1 Marram grass	2 Sea pink
3 Sea lettuce	4 Bladderwrack

FOR YOU TO WRITE

Fill in the missing words yourself.

1 . . . . . roots hold the sand together.
2 The . . . . . grows on rocks and cliffs.
3 The sea pink has pink . . . . .
4 . . . . . plants have no roots, stems or leaves.
5 . . . . . have no flowers.
6 . . . . . is a green sea plant.
7 . . . . . is a brown sea plant.

MARRAM GRASS
ON SANDHILLS

SEA PINK
ON CLIFFS

BLADDERS

SEA LETTUCE
ON ROCKY SHORES

BLADDERWRACK
ON ALL SHORES

FOR YOU TO DO

1 Tear the leaf of a land plant.
  Tear a piece of bladderwrack. See how tough it is.
  Find its bladders. Can you pop one?
2 Look for bubbles on a sea lettuce plant.
3 Look for other kinds of sea plants.
4 Look for other kinds of land plants on the sandhills.
  See if you can find a dandelion there.

35

LIVING ANIMALS BY THE SEA

* The seal is a mammal that lives in the sea.
  We do not often see the seal.
  It likes wild rocky places on the coast.
  It feeds on fish.
* Gulls are birds which live by the sea.
  Sometimes they come inland for food.
  Sometimes their food is dead.
  Sometimes it is alive.
  They feed on both plant and animal foods.
* Many kinds of fish live in the sea.
  They swim too far away for us to see them.
  We can see the goby.
  It is a little fish that lives in rocky pools.
  It feeds on tiny living animals.
  Its two front fins make a little sucker.
* Insects do not live in the sea.
  There are not very many that live on the beach.
  The seaweed fly is one we may see.
  It feeds on the seaweed left on the sand.

FOR YOU TO DRAW

1 A seal   2 A gull   3 A goby   4 A seaweed fly

FOR YOU TO WRITE

Fill in the missing words yourself.

1 The seal is a . . . . . living in the sea.
2 The seal feeds on . . . . .
3 . . . . . feed on animal and plant foods.
4 Sometimes their food is . . . . . ; sometimes alive.
5 The goby lives in rocky . . . . .
6 The seaweed fly feeds on . . . . . on the . . . . . .
7 . . . . . do not live in the sea.

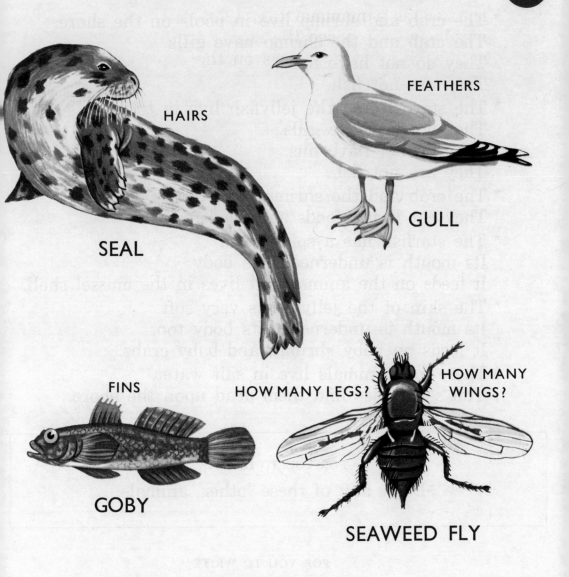

SEAL — HAIRS

GULL — FEATHERS

FINS — GOBY

HOW MANY LEGS? — HOW MANY WINGS? — SEAWEED FLY

FOR YOU TO DO

1 Different kinds of gulls have different markings.
  See how many different kinds you can see.
2 Watch gulls feeding. Find out what they eat.
3 Look at the beaks and feet of gulls.
4 Ask a fisherman the names of the fish he catches.
5 Look for insects on the rocks and in the sandhills.

36

OTHER ANIMALS ON THE SHORE

* The crab and shrimp live in pools on the shore.
  The crab and the shrimp have gills.
  They do not have fins.
  They are not fish.
* The starfish and the jellyfish live in the sea.
  They do not have gills.
  They do not have fins.
  They are not fish.
* The crab and the shrimp have crusty skins.
  They eat living foods and dead foods.
* The starfish has a spiny skin.
  Its mouth is underneath its body.
  It feeds on the animal that lives in the mussel shell.
* The skin of the jellyfish is very soft.
  Its mouth is underneath its body too.
  It feeds on baby shrimps and baby crabs.
* These four animals live in salt water.
  You sometimes find them dead upon the shore.

FOR YOU TO DRAW

Draw any of these 'other' animals.

FOR YOU TO WRITE

Fill in the missing words for yourself.

1 The crab and the shrimp have . . . . . skins.
2 They have . . . . . to breathe under water.
3 They are not fish; they have no . . . . .
4 The starfish has a . . . . . skin.
5 The skin of the . . . . . is very soft.
6 These animals have no fins; they are not . . . . .

SHORE CRAB

SHRIMP

RAYS

STARFISH

JELLYFISH

FOR YOU TO DO

1 Count the legs of a crab.
  Find out where its eyes are.
2 See if you can count the legs of a shrimp.
3 Count the rays of a starfish.
  These are not legs, but part of the body.
4 A jellyfish may sting. Carry it on a spade to a pool
  of water. Watch it to see if it is still alive.
5 Look for other kinds of animals on the shore.